Original title:
Rhymes of the Rill

Copyright © 2025 Creative Arts Management OÜ
All rights reserved.

Author: Derek Caldwell
ISBN HARDBACK: 978-1-80567-365-1
ISBN PAPERBACK: 978-1-80567-664-5

Melodies of the Brook

The brook sings songs of playful cheer,
Bubbles giggle as they disappear.
Frogs in bow ties croak with flair,
While otters zoom without a care.

Leaves dance lightly on the breeze,
Squirrels play hide and seek with ease.
A beaver with a wooden grin,
Builds hotels for friends within.

Lullabies of the Current

The current hums a tune so sweet,
As fish parade in their finned feet.
Turtles nap upon a log,
While crickets sing a night-time fog.

A raccoon dreams of berry pie,
And owls hoot jokes that make one sigh.
Stars wink down from skies so wide,
All creatures laugh at the moonlit tide.

Serenade of the Shallows

In the shallows, laughter flows,
With minnows dancing in a row.
A heron whispers silly snaps,
As turtles share their funny maps.

Water lilies sport sun hats,
As dragonflies perform their mats.
The breeze tells tales that make you smile,
In the shallows where joy is a style.

Ballads Beneath the Bridge

Beneath the bridge, the echoes play,
Where fish tell tales of silly sway.
A raccoon strums a twig guitar,
Singing about adventures afar.

The shadows giggle, ghosts of fun,
As echoes laugh in the setting sun.
A splash, a wiggle, a funny song,
In the river, the joy stays strong.

Soliloquy of the Stream

Bubbles giggle, splashes sing,
A fish in a hat, what a funny thing!
With currents swirling, it loves to dance,
Jumping from rocks, oh what a prance!

The turtles chuckle, the frogs all grin,
A race with the wind, let's begin!
They tumble and tumble, oh what a sight,
Chasing each other till the fall of night.

The sneaky otter steals a shoe,
What will he do with that, who knew?
As branches sway, and leaves take flight,
They're all just laughing, what a delight!

The water's tales, they ripple and flow,
Of witty fish fights, and tides that glow.
With every splash, a joke is spun,
The stream keeps flowing, it's always fun!

Tales of the Teeming Thicket

In the thicket, where laughter roams,
Squirrels wear glasses and build tiny homes.
The rabbits debate, who hops the best,
While owls roll their eyes, and take a rest.

A hedgehog plays tunes on an old tin can,
While crickets dance, forming a band.
The bushes are swaying, chuckling low,
As bees join in, putting on a show.

The wise old fox tells tall tales galore,
Of treasure maps and adventures in store.
The bushes erupt with giggles and squeaks,
For every tall tale, there's mischief that peaks!

The thicket's alive, with fun and with cheer,
With stories that echo, crystal clear.
Amidst all the hustle, the playful thrill,
Nature's own comedy, mirth of the hill!

The Heritage of Waters

In a brook where the fish like to play,
The chatter flows bright, night and day.
A frog with a hat croaks a tune,
While ducks form a band under the moon.

Splashing is rampant, oh what a sight,
Where water's a stage and laughter's the light.
The turtles join in with a comical glide,
As bubbles rise up on this wild, merry ride.

Purling Narratives

A stream weaves stories, some silly, some sweet,
With pebbles as characters, quite hard to beat.
A snail wears a tie, so dapper and fine,
While minnows debate who'll dance on the line.

The current brings whispers of tales yet untold,
Of pirate fish ships and treasure of gold.
With giggles of gurgles, they share all their dreams,
As the water sparkles and bubbles in beams.

The Saga of the Swirling Stream

Oh romp and oh roll, the currents entwine,
As fish do the cha-cha, and ebbs sip their wine.
A beaver in braces builds homes with a grin,
While otters are surfing, oh where to begin!

With ricocheting splashes and dramatic dips,
The waterway's wild, with twists and flips.
Each ripple a laugh from a gathering scene,
Where joy flows like water, both fresh and serene.

The Dance of the Drifting Leaf

A leaf on the water starts twirling around,
It dances with grace, never making a sound.
With a wink and a spin, it catches a breeze,
While droplets applaud with a splash of their tease.

It tumbles and sways, a waltz with the flow,
As willows lean in, enjoying the show.
With each little dip comes a giggle or two,
Oh, the joy of the journey, how splendidly true!

Melodies of the Wandering Waters

The river danced with a silly grin,
It splashed at ducks and invited them in.
Fish flipped over, their scales a bright hue,
Singing fish tales that nobody knew.

With bubbles that floated like balloons in the air,
The frogs joined in, croaking without a care.
Water skippers joked, racing here and there,
While the turtles snoozed, dreaming without a dare.

Serenade of the Silver Current

The silver stream pouted, it lost a good race,
Against a pebble that took off with grace.
Laughter erupted from reeds lining the shore,
As it swirled in circles, wanting much more.

A snail slipped past in a slow-motion waltz,
While a fish tried to dance and gave it a jolt.
Splashing jokes flew like leaves in the breeze,
As the water chuckled with delightful unease.

Chants of the Tinkling Tides

The tides sang out in a tickling tone,
So playful and light, they made seashells moan.
"Catch us if you can!" the waves seemed to shout,
While seagulls laughed and circled about.

The tide pools echoed with giggles so bright,
As starfish whispered, "We're creatures of night!"
Crabs did a jig on the slippery sand,
Turning the shore into a dance party grand.

Ballads by the Babbling Fountain

A fountain bubbled, bursting with cheer,
Its water like laughter, drawing all near.
Squirrels interrupted with antics so sly,
While pigeons cooed, wearing scruffy neckties.

Each splash told a story, a chuckle, a grin,
Bantering with bubbles that danced with a spin.
"Bet you can't catch this!" the fountain did tease,
As giggles erupted in the soft summer breeze.

The Water's Tender Soliloquy

A brook babbles softly, without a care,
It tickles the rocks, tickles the air.
Fish gossip below, in a glimmering spree,
While frogs croak in laughter, 'Hey, look at me!'

With splashes and giggles, the waves take flight,
The pebbles chuckle, 'Ain't this a sight?'
A snail hums a tune, creeping along slow,
While the breeze sings a ditty that nobody knows.

Flowing Thoughts in Liquid Prose

Here flows a stream, with stories to share,
Whispers of reeds sway in the air.
A turtle wears glasses, reads by the shore,
His book's full of tales that have never been bore.

A fish in a hat tries to catch some sun,
Dancing to gurgles, he's the life of the fun.
Water skimmers swoop in a fussy array,
Telling the current, 'You're speeding away!'

A Dance of Drifting Melodies

Raindrops drop gently, with a cheeky sound,
They tap on the leaves, in a merry round.
A duck on a quest, wearing boots quite bold,
Squeaks, 'I'm an explorer - come join, be told!'

The bubbles erupt with a fizzy delight,
They splatter and soar, in a giggly flight.
Currents sway softly, a liquid ballet,
With laughter from crickets that seem to replay.

Ebb and Flow of Feelings

Waves roll in gently, with a wink and a grin,
They tickle the sand, teasing the skin.
A starfish spins tales, with arms spread so wide,
While clams whisper secrets of the ocean's pride.

The tide pulls and pushes, in playful delight,
As seagulls squawk jokes, taking flight in the light.
The moon winks down, with a luminescent glow,
Saying, 'Life's a big splash, let's put on a show!'

The Soft Symphony of Silken Waters

In a brook where fish do prance,
The frogs all sing, they love to dance.
With splashes here and splashes there,
The water sings of joy and flair.

A turtle wearing fancy hats,
Pauses by to check the chats.
He nods his head to beats so grand,
The splish-splash band at his command.

The bubbles rise with every joke,
Each ripple laughs, the air's a cloak.
The dragonflies all giggle too,
They flutter here with skies so blue.

Oh, what a scene of jolly fun,
With all of nature on the run.
The water's tune, it makes us smile,
A silly song, let's stay awhile.

Cadence of the Cascading Falls

Down the cliff, the waters rush,
They tumble down with mighty hush.
A fish jumps up, it aims to fly,
Splashing down as birds swoop by.

The rocks below all wear a grin,
As raindrops fall, they leap and spin.
Each drop an artist with a splash,
Creating art in every crash.

The otters join in, full of glee,
Sledding down the banks, oh me!
They slide right in but make a fumble,
A watery twist, oh how they tumble!

With every splash, the giggles flow,
Under the sun's warm golden glow.
As laughter rings, they dance and fall,
The joyous tune of nature's call.

Reflections in a Splash of Stanzas

In puddles deep, the sky reflects,
While ducks parade in quirky texts.
Feet tromp about, with splashes wide,
As fancies swim on gleeful tide.

The sunbeam giggles, shines so bright,
It sparks the dance of day to night.
The willows chuckle as they sway,
In rhythms sweet, they softly play.

A fish with dreams of daring feats,
Wads through the water, cheeky treats.
With every wiggle, each new prank,
He flips and flops with boaters plank.

The melody of splashes loud,
Invites us all to join the crowd.
So come and clap; it's quite a scene,
Where every droplet's part of the routine.

Rhythms from the Riverbed

Among the pebbles, gurgles play,
With tiny fish that dash and sway.
The rhythm echoes, soft and sweet,
With every pulse, they skip their beat.

The mossy stones all whisper tales,
Of silly winds and sneaky gales.
A crab in boots, he struts with pride,
As waves applaud from every side.

The ripples form a lively crew,
As reeds all sway to dance anew.
A far-off splash, the frogs reply,
With croaks and laughs that fill the sky.

So gather round, don't miss the show,
In nature's choir, let your heart grow.
With giggles shared, the water smiles,
Join in the fun; it's worth your while.

The Dance of Eddies

The water spins with playful glee,
As fish wear hats and dance with me.
The bubbles laugh and churn around,
While turtles groove without a sound.

A frog jumps high and strikes a pose,
He cracks a joke and then he goes.
The current twirls, the splashy beat,
With every turn, it's quite a treat.

The dragonflies join in the fun,
With tiny wings, they're on the run.
They zip and zoom, a circus show,
In nature's dance, we steal the glow.

So come along, enjoy the spree,
Where laughter lives in every spree.
The dance of eddies, bright and bold,
With water tales yet to be told.

Phrases in Poolside Harmony

At the pool, the splashes play,
With rubber ducks in wild array.
A cannonball makes quite a splash,
While kids all giggle, hearts unabashed.

The sun wears shades and laughs aloud,
As beach balls bounce without a shroud.
A swimming race turns into fun,
With floaties racing, one by one.

The sunblock game, a treasure hunt,
With faces smeared, not a hint of blunt.
While water slides twist and swirl,
The splash zone sings, let laughter unfurl!

So poolside dreams are light and free,
With jokes and antics, glee's the key.
In this wet world, we share a smile,
And poolside phrases stretch for miles.

Dreaming in the Drift

In drifting dreams, the leaves take flight,
A funny swirl in morning light.
The river winks, a playful tease,
Where wishes dance upon the breeze.

A fish in glasses scales the stream,
As jokes take form, we laugh and beam.
The water's voice, a chuckle so sweet,
In nature's drift, we find our beat.

The clouds parade with silly shapes,
While water's edge turns into tapes.
A gopher slides with style and flair,
In dreamy drifts, there's laughter everywhere!

So join the flow and drift along,
In silly streams, we all belong.
With every twist, our spirits lift,
In dreamy drifts, there's joy to gift.

The Sonnet of the Streambed

The streambed sings a comic tune,
With stones like frogs, they'll dance by noon.
A beaver builds a cozy den,
While wise old rocks just smile at men.

The otters slide with glee and grace,
In silly games, they take their place.
With laughter on the water's tongue,
In sonnets made, our hearts are sprung.

A heron jokes with every stride,
While turtles wait upon the tide.
With rippling rhymes, the moments blend,
In streambed tales, the fun won't end.

So let's rejoice in nature's jest,
Where water flows and laughter's best.
In every twist, we see the fun,
The sonnet sung, 'til day is done.

Songs of the Wandering Waters

A frog on a log sings so loud,
His voice draws a curious crowd.
The fish start to dance with delight,
While turtles just watch, what a sight!

The river keeps chuckling with glee,
Tickling the toes of a bumblebee.
A splash from a splashy old rat,
Who quips, 'Where's my hat? Where's my hat?'

With each twist, the water does flow,
It carries old leaves, a fine show.
The ducks laugh and try to keep pace,
While swans strike a pose in the race!

So here's to the streams, forever in jest,
Life's silly moments, they weave with the best.
Float on, little bubbles, with joy and with thrill,
For laughter is born where the waters stand still!

The Gentle Song of the Stream

A pebble falls with a plunk,
The little fish giggles, what junk!
Water tickles the toes of the shore,
While crabs in the sand try to dance more!

The leaves wiggle as if to the beat,
While frogs tap their feet to the heat.
The splash of a bird takes flight,
As it tries to join in on the fun, what a sight!

A snail took a stroll, oh so slow,
Singing a tune that nobody knows.
The ripples respond with a wink,
Nature's mad laughter, the best way to think!

So raise your cups to the babbling stream,
Where giggles and gurgles create a dream.
With water so merry, let's all sing along,
Join in the chorus, a bubbly song!

Currents of a Dream

A busy old beaver builds up a dam,
While a raccoon plots, cooking up a jam.
Fish wiggle and giggle with mirth,
While turtles flip coins, playing games of worth!

The bubbles go pop, like silly balloons,
As dragonflies dance to the wild tunes.
Each wave has a story, a chuckle, a cheer,
Wobbling like jelly, oh, what a dear!

The sun smiles down with a twinkle and wink,
As frogs crack up, causing a stink.
The current sings loud, with quips that delight,
Making the moments so very bright!

So splash in the water, join in the fun,
Where laughter flows free, and troubles are none.
Under the bright sky, let your spirit scream,
Life is a giggle, and we're part of the dream!

Nature's Softest Serenade

Whispers of ripples crawl through the night,
As owls hoot softly, under starlight.
A rabbit hops by, with a wink and a grin,
While shadows of trees play hide and seek within.

The moon laughs bright, shining silver and round,
As crickets compose, a sweet, tiny sound.
A squirrel in pajamas, now isn't that neat?
Starts a conga line, can you handle the beat?

The winds swirl around like a playful ghost,
Telling the tales of the things we love most.
With flowers that giggle, and leaves that refrain,
Nature's a stage for this twilight entertain!

So sing with the waters, let joy take its flight,
With each note of humor that glimmers at night.
In the dance of the leaves, the songbirds convene,
Where laughter is woven, so bright and serene!

Watercolor Whimsy

In splashes bright, the colors dance,
The fish wear ties, they love to prance.
With every ripple, a giggle's found,
As ducks play poker, all around.

The frogs wear crowns, they rule the shores,
While turtles race, with tiny roars.
A snail in shades takes quite a stroll,
While bubbling laughter fills the hole.

The dragonflies buzz in silly hats,
Chasing their dreams, like acrobats.
While water fowl tell knock-knock jokes,
Amid the reeds, where joy evokes.

So here we splash, with bubbles bold,
Painting laughter, as stories unfold.
The stream is bright with humor's thrill,
Where nature giggles, and hearts are still.

A Symphony of Stillness

A gentle breeze, the leaves all sway,
While crickets hum in their own way.
The frogs join in, a croaking beat,
As fireflies dance on tiny feet.

A turtle's leap is full of glee,
He trips and falls—oh, look at me!
The water's calm, but laughs erupt,
As fish hold court, their tales corrupt.

The wind plays notes like a sly old cat,
With whispers sweet and titters flat.
In this serene and funny place,
Nature's humor finds its space.

With every drop, a chuckle stirs,
As tiny creatures waltz like furs.
Their symphony sings through leaves and ground,
An orchestra of laughs all around.

The Stream's Lullaby

The water chuckles as it glides,
With rocks that giggle, joy abides.
A fish with glasses reads a book,
While playful otters soar and nook.

Beneath the bridge, a raccoon snores,
Dreaming of cookies and open doors.
While frogs wear shoes in bright array,
And leap like dancers in their play.

A turtle strums a leafy lute,
With strumming notes that shake the root.
The nightingale joins in with flair,
Singing loudly without a care.

As stars blink down on this sweet sight,
The stream hums soft, with pure delight.
A lullaby that'll make you smile,
As nature winks and stays awhile.

The Graces of the Streamlet

A streamlet giggles in the sun,
Where rocks become a throne for fun.
Tiny fairies, with wings of light,
Throw sparkles in a playful flight.

An eager worm, dressed up in style,
Slides through moss with grace and guile.
While daisies sway in silly dance,
Each petal grinning, as if by chance.

The minnows play tag, swift and spry,
While dragonflies zoom and fly high.
The laughter bubbles, bright and keen,
In this game, they reign supreme.

With every splash, joy takes its course,
In petal boats, they set the source.
The streamlet sings with a chuckle and grin,
Where magic happens, let joy begin.

Songs of Solace in the Stream

A fish wore a hat, quite askew,
It danced with delight, out of the blue.
A snail called it silly, oh what a sight,
They laughed as they twirled in the soft morning light.

A frog on a lily, with dreams of a band,
Played tunes with his toes, how strange and how grand.
The dragonflies giggled, flew high in the air,
As bubbles floated up, without a single care.

Tadpoles in tuxedos swayed to the beat,
While crickets chirped loudly, tapping their feet.
The stream held a party, no worries at all,
With laughter so loud, you'd think it could sprawl.

Down by the brook, where giggles unite,
There's always a jest, there's always delight.
They sing of the joys with a splash and a splash,
In waters so silly, they'll never be brash.

Overture of the Ripple

The water took a spin, with a wink and a grin,
A porcupine joined in, much to his chagrin.
He slipped on a leaf, went tumbling around,
With a splash and a flail, he got up and frowned.

A squirrel on a branch told a joke from afar,
About nuts that could dance, and a moon made of tar.
The fish rolled their eyes, with bubbles of glee,
As the otters all chortled, wild and free.

The wind spun a tale of a whiskered old king,
Who ruled over ripples, oh what a strange fling!
With laughter like music, they swirled in a row,
While frogs played their banjos, giving the flow.

The brook's such a stage, with antics so bright,
Each ripple a curtain, in sun's shining light.
In moments of mirth, let your worries all flee,
Join the raucous celebration by the grand old tree.

Streams of Recollection

In a stream full of memories, odd and absurd,
A turtle recounted, each tale had a word.
Of battles with beavers, and races in dreams,
Of royal raccoons and their elaborate schemes.

A wise old catfish, with whiskers of gold,
Told tales of the days when the water was cold.
"I caught the big one! Oh, what a wild ride!"
While crickets cheered on, they swayed side to side.

The tadpoles took notes, with pencils so keen,
Writing down stories, of places they've been.
A bubble burst suddenly, with giggles so loud,
As memories splashed up, drawing in quite a crowd.

With each little ripple, a story would flow,
In the dance of the stream, where we all set aglow.
Embrace every moment, however they land,
In whimsical waters, together we stand.

Ghosts of the Glimmering Flow

See the ghosts in the water, having a laugh,
One's wearing a top hat, doing the math.
They've lost all their socks, under a rock,
While eels do the twist, and the frogs mock the clock.

The trout are all gossiping, diving for dirt,
About who in the pond wore the silliest shirt.
With feathers and bells, they jingle-jangle,
As the bubbles of joy in the sunlight dangle.

A minnow in glasses, quite scholarly, brash,
Claimed he could read, but just made a splash.
The turtles rolled over, nearly floated away,
As laughter echoed back, through the glorious spray.

For here in this stream, where the fun never ends,
The ghosts meet each dusk, and the giggling transcends.
They play in the glimmer, the water's their show,
In the currents of joy, where the silly winds blow.

Harmonic Ripples

In a pond where frogs will croak,
A fish told a joke, it went up in smoke.
The lily pads giggled, a splashing spree,
As ducks quacked loud, "Just let it be!"

A turtle laughed, took a dive,
Said, "Now that's how we all thrive!"
The bubbles rose with a pop and a cheer,
While water skippers skated near.

The dragonflies danced, in the sun's bright glow,
While minnows swirled in a comical show.
They twirled and whirled in a watery ball,
Said, "Join in, everyone! We're having a ball!"

As the sun set low, the giggles grew,
With each splash and rip, more antics to strew.
Even the reeds swayed to the beat,
With laughter and joy, it's a watery treat!

Ballads of Babbling Brooks

In a brook where the pebbles shone,
A crab told tales of his royal throne.
The minnows snickered, as they passed by,
"Crown or no crown, you only can sigh!"

A squirrel popped down with a nut in hand,
"Do I hear tunes from a mighty band?"
The water sang sweet, a bubbling delight,
With frogs uniting in a karaoke night!

The tall grass swayed, with a chuckle or two,
As fish swam in circles, just to show you.
"Oh, what a life!" a goldfish did smile,
As a heron tripped on a twig in style!

So when you walk by, don't miss the fun,
For the brook is alive, with laughter spun.
Each splash and ripple, a tale to tell,
In the ballad of babbles, all's going well!

The Whispering Waters

The creek had secrets, giggled all day,
As fish whispered tales in a watery sway.
A turtle wore glasses, so wise and grand,
"I saw that big splash! Can you give me a hand?"

The rocks chuckled back, with echoes so bright,
As frogs on the bank exclaimed, "What a sight!"
A dragonfly danced on whispers of breeze,
"Catch me if you can, I'm harder to seize!"

With each little bubble that surfaced to play,
The water's soft joy was a fun-filled display.
The sun set the stage for a shimmering glow,
As the creek laughed softly, its jokes in tow.

So come take a dip in the secrets profound,
With giggles and gurgles, let laughter abound.
For the whispers of water will lighten your heart,
In a world where each splash is a humorous art!

Choral Echoes of the Streambed

In a stream where the pebbles chime,
A chorus of frogs found their rhythm in time.
With a ribbit and croak, they formed a great band,
Each note echoed back, in synchrony grand.

A fish twirled around with a sparkly grin,
Exclaimed, "I'm the star! Now let's begin!"
The wind joined in with a merry soft tune,
As ants gathered 'round in the light of the moon.

The willows started swaying, their leaves in delight,
While crickets composed in the coolness of night.
The water sang back, a harmony sweet,
While the starlight danced on with a shimmering beat.

So join in the laughter, the music, the cheer,
For the echoes of joy, you'll hear loud and clear.
In the choral streambed, where stories abound,
Every splash brings laughter, and happiness found!

Dances in the Dew

In the morning light, they prance,
Tiny bugs take a dance.
With wiggly wobbles on the grass,
They giggle, 'Oh, how we pass!'

Droplets hold a bouncing ball,
As each little bug feels small.
With a splash, they take a dive,
Their jigs make the flowers thrive.

The sun joins in with a bright grin,
While leaves sway, let the fun begin!
Now a puddle joins the crew,
What a party, just for you!

So join the insects, take a leap,
In the dew, humor is deep.
With laughter in the morning's glow,
Dancing dew drops steal the show!

The Melody of the Mellow Stream

In a flow that hums and sings,
Little fish wear make-believe wings.
They splash about with wiggly flair,
Underneath the bridge, there's a fish fair!

The turtles chuckle, spin around,
In this gurgling joy, no frown is found.
With bubbles giggling and swirls so bright,
The stream's melody feels just right.

Frogs croak out a silly tune,
Under the soft gaze of the moon.
They tap their feet on river rocks,
Adding rhythm, ticking clocks.

So let the waters tickle your ears,
With splashes that bring you cheers.
Mellow streams with laughter embrace,
While nature wears a happy face!

Voices Among the Rocks

Whispers bounce off rugged stones,
Where the lizards make their tones.
They chirp in chatty little packs,
With pebble pals and funny cracks.

A gentle breeze joins in the fun,
Tickling edges, everyone's spun.
The crickets join, with legs that click,
Creating raucous, silly tricks.

The owls hoot, but in a jest,
How many voices? They're all a fest!
Rocks giggle with their stone-cold laughter,
In this echo, joy comes after.

So if you wander where it's wild,
Listen close as nature smiled.
Voices play, in harmony,
Among the rocks, pure jubilee!

The Lure of the Liquid Lane

Wiggly waters twist and turn,
A river's giggle makes us yearn.
It tickles toes, a splashy shoe,
In playful waves, oh what a view!

Rubber ducks bob, oh so bright,
Their quacks echo in pure delight.
They race the current, side by side,
With giggles flowing like a tide.

Here come the frogs, with leaps so spry,
Jumping high beneath the sky.
In a splashdown, what a cheer,
Funny friends are gathered here.

So take a dip in fun's embrace,
In liquid lanes, you'll find your place.
With laughter ringing loud and clear,
The lure of water brings you cheer!

Verses of the Velvet Tide

A fish in a tie said, "Oh my, oh my!"
He danced on the shore, with a wink in his eye.
The crabs had a giggle, they snapped at the light,
While turtles in top hats prepared for a fight.

A seagull sang tunes, quite off-key and silly,
While dolphins played tag, oh so fast and frilly.
The waves went on laughing, a frothy good cheer,
As shells shared their secrets, no sign of mere fear.

Barnacles whispered, 'We've seen it all, mate!'
As oysters in pearls held a party so great.
The sun threw a party, with rays soft and wide,
These creatures of water enjoyed every ride.

So come to the edge, where the fun never ends,
With fishy dictators and octopus friends.
In the belly of laughter, let's paddle and glide,
In the joy of the wave, where the sea-breeze'll guide.

Notes from the Nymph's Cove

In the cove where nymphs twirl, with glee they confide,
They pull up their skirts with a giggle and glide.
A frog croaks a tune, so silly and bold,
While fish mimic dancers, a sight to behold.

The water's a mirror, reflecting the fun,
As splashes of laughter and bubbles are spun.
They weave through the reeds, wearing crowns of pure foam,
And sing silly jingles, 'We're far from our home!'

A crab tried to salsa, but slipped on a shell,
The bubbles erupted, oh, what a smell!
The nymphs burst with laughter; they rolled in the grass,
As the lilies all blushed, letting joy overflow fast.

So if you should wander to this cove of delight,
You'll find not just nymphs, but a marvelous sight.
With giggles and wiggles, the echoes still roam,
In the waters of laughter, you'll finally feel home.

Flowing Dreams

In a stream where dreams twinkle and glimmer like stars,
A fish told a tale of jellybean cars.
They zoomed past the bubbles, quite fancy and bright,
As frogs in tuxedos yelled, 'What a delight!'

The crickets held concerts, their rhythm was sweet,
While turtles beat-boxed to quite a fast beat.
A party of currents made waves and replaced,
The worries of land with a splash and a haste.

With snails in their shellphones, they chimed in a beat,
Singing songs of the river, a cha-cha retreat.
The banks shook with laughter, a joyous parade,
As the fish played the tuba, the crabs were dismayed.

So drift with the currents where giggles delight,
In flowing concoctions of silliness bright.
The whimsy will guide you, just follow the stream,
Where even the sillies can dance in a dream.

The Water's Cadence

Down by the brook, where the water is free,
A giant named Splash said, "Come play with me!"
With splashes and giggles, the fish took the stage,
While ducks quacked in rhythm, they joyfully gage.

The sun made a point to join in on the fun,
As the river danced under the warmth of its run.
The turtles wore shades, looking oh-so-cool,
While a clam in a boa played the fool.

A bubble parade had the frogs on the hop,
With lily pads flying, they couldn't stop.
The laughter echoed, a melodic retreat,
As the water clapped hands and gave them a beat.

So if ever you wander where giggles abound,
You'll find humor and harmony spinning around.
In the cascade of cheer, let your cares finally fade,
In the rhythm of water, find joy unafraid.

The Beckoning of the Bank

Down by the stream, ducks play tag,
Waddling around like a silly rag.
Frogs croak loud with a hearty cheer,
Splashing about, oh dear, oh dear!

A fisherman slips with a splashy flop,
His rod goes flying, a real big drop!
The fish just giggle, then swim away,
Leaving our friend in disarray.

Squirrels gather, chattering near,
Munching acorns, full of cheer.
One takes a dive, who knew it could fall?
Into the water, they all break the thrall!

And as the sun twinkles on the tide,
Each little creature takes life in stride.
Laughs echo wild in the bubbling brook,
The bank's alive, let's take a look!

Images in Rippling Waters

A silver fish dons a fancy hat,
While turtles chill, oh, how they chat!
A dragonfly zooms in with a twist,
"Did you see that?" it says with a hiss!

The water plays tricks, look at that swirl,
A boy tries to fish but gives it a whirl!
His line gets tangled, oh what a show,
The fish swim by, laughing below.

With a splash and a splash, they dance with glee,
While the wise old frog croaks, "That's life, you see?
Just go with the flow, don't fight the tide,
For sometimes, in chaos, you'll find your stride."

As shadows grow long and laughter dims,
The lake sparkles bright with whimsical whims.
And so we watch, with a chuckle or two,
At images bright, in the water's view!

Cascading Harmonies

A waterfall sings while rocks keep beat,
Fish twirl around, oh what a feat!
The breeze joins in, with a soft little whine,
Nature's orchestra, perfectly in line.

A raccoon joins in with mismatched paws,
Sipping the water and giving applause.
While otters slide down in giddy delight,
Their giggles echo into the night.

A wayward twig starts a ruckus, oh my!
As it floats downstream, a very fine spy!
The critters all ponder where it might go,
Turns out it was just a show for the show!

With splashes and laughter, the currents entwine,
A symphony echoes, all fluid and fine.
In this cheerful dance where all creatures bloom,
Nature's sweet giggles banish all gloom!

Rivulets of Recollection

Memories trickle down the bank with glee,
Where past moments dance like leaves in a spree.
The laughter of children heard on the breeze,
Echoes of joy, a heart's sweet tease.

Old gnarled trees share stories untold,
Of days long gone, full of daring bold.
The water wraps tales in its gentle embrace,
As shadows of youth find a new place.

Frogs croak out tunes of a softer time,
While crickets provide a rhythm and rhyme.
The sun casts a glow on this rippling array,
Reminders of laughter that never decay.

As we sit by the bank and reminisce,
The bubbles of joy foreshadow a kiss.
With chuckles and whispers, time flows on through,
In rivulets sparkling, memories renew!

The Stream's Gentle Sighs

A brook runs by with playful glee,
It tickles rocks, just wait and see.
Frogs leap in with joyful croaks,
While fish roll eyes at the silly folks.

The pebbles dance in swirling jest,
As bubbles rise, they fail the test.
A splash of water on a shoe,
It's all in fun, what can you do?

Leaves drift down like silly hats,
Carried off by splashing spats.
A dragonfly zooms, what a show!
He twirls and dips in the flow.

A picnic spread on the grassy side,
But ants invade, they take a ride!
With laughter loud and giggles bright,
The stream keeps flowing, pure delight.

Chronicles of the Blue Current

The river sings with a cheeky grin,
Whirls and swirls as it pulls you in.
A turtle rides like a tiny boat,
While minnows nibble on his coat.

Sticks float by, a parade of fun,
Competing for attention, all in the run.
A duck pirouettes with a splashy flair,
While nearby, a fish is caught unaware.

With echoes of laughter, the banks do shake,
As kids toss stones, oh, the splashes they make!
A crab waves claws in a funny dance,
Inviting all for a water chance.

Even a log attempts to play,
With splintered limbs and a mossy sway.
In this tale of a wiggling stream,
Life's a laugh, a playful dream.

The Ballad of Waters Sprung

A fountain bursts with a joyful cheer,
Water flies high, far and near.
Children giggle as they rush close,
Daring droplets, more than a boast.

The wind gives chase, a comical race,
It tugs at hats, the silliest case.
While ducks form a line without a care,
Quacking rhythms in the air.

A beaver builds in a clumsy spree,
While frogs strike poses as models, you see.
Each plop, each splash, a tickle of fun,
Under the warmth of the shining sun.

As night creeps in, the glowworms play,
Lighting up the brook in a charming display.
With laughter echoing all around,
In the ballad of waters, joy is found.

Ballads as they Wander

A babbling brook hums a merry tune,
As it wanders by the light of the moon.
With stones that giggle when disturbed,
And currents dancing, gently curbed.

A heron trips on its own two feet,
Stumbles and falls, what a funny feat!
As minnows snicker, they hide and peek,
In this watery world, it's laughter we seek.

The creek meanders, a jester bold,
With tales of giggles waiting to unfold.
Each twist and turn, a playful bend,
Where nature's humor is sure to send.

And as the sun dips low and shy,
Reflections shimmer, dances comply.
In these ballads, as they drift and sway,
Wander with joy, come laugh and play.

Odes to the Swaying Leaves

As leaves in breezes start to dance,
They twirl and spin, a leafy prance.
The trees all chuckle, what a sight,
In nature's folly, pure delight.

With acorns falling, they slip and slide,
A nutty game they cannot hide.
The squirrels laugh as they embark,
To catch their treasures in the park.

A beetle joins, he winks with glee,
"Come join us for a jamboree!"
The wind blows harder, what a tease,
In this grand party of the leaves.

With every rustle, secrets told,
Of playful tales that never grow old.
So sway along, you merry crew,
For nature's jesters, that is you!

Cadence of the Cascade

Oh water's leap, like frogs in race,
From stone to stone, you find your place.
You giggle and chuckle, splash and spray,
Turning stones to glimmering clay.

"Oh look at me!" a pebble cried,
As he slipped down the waterfall slide.
With every drop, a joke unfurls,
The brook a stage for nature's twirls.

A fish swims by, gives a wink,
"Let's flip and flop, what do you think?"
They dive and dance, a watery jig,
Making ripples, small and big.

So when you hear the babbling song,
Remember laughter floats along.
In every splash, let joy cascade,
In nature's stream, we laugh and wade!

The Trickle's Tale

Once a trickle, not quite a stream,
Had dreams of grandeur, oh how they gleam.
With every flick, a story spills,
Of silly ducks and joyful thrills.

A pebble grumbled, "I'm stuck, I swear!"
As the trickle laughed and gave a dare.
"Don't be shy, just roll with me,
We'll make it far, you'll see, you'll see!"

Tiny tadpoles join the fun,
They swirl around, a water run.
"Catch me if you can!" they croak and dive,
In this merry race, they feel alive.

So listen close, to the gentle sound,
Of water's wisdom, all around.
In every trickle, life's a tale,
With laughter flowing, will prevail!

Murmurs of the Deep

In depths of blue, where bubbles rise,
The fish have secrets, oh what a prize!
With fins a-flutter, they play a game,
Of peek-a-boo, oh such fame!

A starfish giggles, a shellfish sighs,
As currents swirl, they improvise.
"Why did the octopus cross the floor?
To stretch its legs! Let's give a roar!"

The seaweed sways with rhythm and cheer,
A pirate's jig that we all hold dear.
"Join in the dance!" the dolphins yell,
In the ocean's playground, all is swell.

So dive below, where laughter reigns,
In murky waters, joy remains.
For even down deep, where it's dark and steep,
The ocean giggles, in bubbles it keeps!

Nature's Verse in Shimmering Shades

In dresses green, the trees do sway,
They giggle softly, come out to play.
The leaves are dancing, twirling round,
While critters laugh upon the ground.

A squirrel's tail twitches with delight,
Chasing shadows in morning light.
Bees hum a tune, oh so absurd,
A rapping rhythm, without a word.

Clouds play tag in a sky so blue,
Winking at each other, a silly crew.
The flowers nod in a quirky spree,
As nature's jesters, wild and free.

With colors bright, all nature's cheer,
Find joy in moments, year to year.
Laughter echoes in every glade,
Nature's verse, in sunlight laid.

Songs of the Silent Stream

The stream whispers secrets, oh so bright,
With fish that giggle, what a sight!
The rocks all chuckle, worn and wise,
While frogs croak jokes underneath the skies.

A leaf sails by, a tiny boat,
While turtles giggle, taking note.
The ripples dance a silly jig,
Each splash a laugh, each bubble big.

Dragonflies flirt, like little sprites,
Buzzing about in nature's nights.
They tease the fish and twirl away,
While frogs break into laughter's play.

Thus the stream flows, never shy,
With songs of giggles, rolling by.
In silence deep, the fun's not missed,
In every splash, the joy persists.

The Fluidity of Unspoken Words

A breeze blows softly, a chuckle shared,
With whispers of leaves, all paired and paired.
The flowers nod with a knowing grin,
As petals dance, let the fun begin.

The wind tells jokes to the wandering trees,
Rustling leaves, laughter floats with ease.
In this quiet chat, they choreograph,
Their playful banter, a nature laugh.

Clouds murmur puns high above the ground,
While shadows stretch, giggling all around.
In every rustle, in every sway,
Unspoken tales of a funny day.

The brook babbles forth a cheeky rhyme,
Its water ripples in perfect time.
Nature's jesters, in a wordless play,
Create their humor, come what may.

Echoing Lullabies of the Bay

The bay hums tunes, its voice so smooth,
With seagulls laughing, in playful grooves.
Waves clap their hands, in jubilant glee,
As crabs do the cha-cha, just wait and see!

Each splash is a joke, retold anew,
As fish dance around in a shimmering crew.
Barnacles chuckle, glued to their spot,
While shells share a secret, funny or not.

The sun dips low, painting the night,
Stars wink playfully, oh what a sight!
Ripples echo echoes of laughter long,
As the bay sings sweetly its own silly song.

In this haven where joy flows free,
Nature's lullabies are meant to be.
With each gentle wave, the humor stays,
In the heart of the fun-loving bay.

Harmonies of the Flow

In the stream where the ducks wear hats,
They paddle in style, avoiding the spats.
A fish sings a tune with its bubbly swish,
Chorusing loudly, 'Hey, did you wish?'

The frogs on the banks hold a lively debate,
About who can jump higher and who's really great.
With croaks that are swift and slippery slides,
They laugh as they bounce, with their froggy guides.

The turtles recline, just taking a nap,
They miss all the fun, warm sun on their lap.
But when they awake, they'll join in the jest,
And race with the current, oh what a quest!

As the water flows on, the giggles don't cease,
Each splash is a punchline, laughter's increase.
With bubbles and ripples, the joy's never still,
In this jolly abode of the happy rill.

Rippled Reflections

Here in the shallows where minnows gleam,
There's a splishy-splash party, the funniest theme.
A squirrel drops acorns, they plop with a sound,
Creating a rhythm that bounces around.

Great grinning geese waddle along the shore,
With stories that twist, they can't wait to score.
Each flap of their wings shakes the laughter free,
While folks at the picnic just grin with glee.

The dragonflies dance in their glittering flare,
Like fairies in flight, they twirl through the air.
Making light of the breeze as they flutter on by,
Whispering secrets that make the lake sigh.

As sunlight dips low and shadows grow long,
The ripples sing sweetly, a cheerful song.
With giggles and splashes, the night soon appears,
Let's toast to the fun, with joy and with cheers!

Songs of the Silver Stream

The silver stream giggles, with frothy delight,
While crickets join in with their chirping at night.
With a splash and a glimmer, the water does sway,
Singing funny tales in its bubbly ballet.

A rabbit pops by, all dressed up in style,
He's wearing a bowtie, he hasn't trotted a mile.
With a wink and a grin, he hops to the beat,
Swaying to songs that no one can cheat.

A family of otters slides down a log,
They giggle and laugh, quite the merry frog.
Playing peek-a-boo with the leaves overhead,
While the moon starts to rise, their fun's just widespread.

As the night fills with laughter and twinkles abound,
The stream just keeps rolling, no end to be found.
With splashes and giggles, it continues to gleam,
In the heart of the night, it fulfills every dream.

Chants of the Cascades

At the foot of the waterfall, what a view!
With bubbles like giggles, the water laughs too.
It tumbles and jingles, a cascading cheer,
While gnomes around gather, all ears, full of cheer.

The plants do a dance, waving leaves in delight,
Joining in on the fun with the stars shining bright.
A choir of crickets, they chirp as they play,
Creating a symphony as night meets the day.

The raccoons in masks, with their paws waving wide,
Join in on the antics, nowhere to hide.
With tails upturned, they prance to and fro,
As the cascades giggle, putting on quite the show.

So gather your friends, let the merriment swell,
With giggles and splashes, let's ring every bell.
For the joy of the water, the fun's never done,
In the chants of the cascades, we all are as one.

Harmonies from Nature's Veins

A squirrel in a hat, quite absurd,
Chirps loudly, no one's heard.
Dancing under trees so green,
What a sight, a wacky scene!

The brook begins to giggle, oh!
As frogs don tap shoes, to and fro.
The breeze plays flute, birds take a stand,
Together they form a silly band!

A leaf floats by on a sunlit wave,
It winks at the fish, oh so brave!
Swirling with joy, they twist and slide,
In this nature's circus, let's all abide!

Even clouds above can't stop their glee,
They puff up like balls, come watch the spree.
With splashes of laughter, chirps in the air,
Nature's own jesters, beyond compare!

The Lure of Liquid Lyrics

A fish with glasses, wise and spry,
Ponders the secrets of the sky.
With tales to tell in bubbling tones,
He can't help giggling, perhaps overblown.

The river, a rambler, tells a pun,
Winding and twisting, all in good fun.
Jumping with laughter, it splashes around,
Sharing its joy with the land it found.

Tiny boats hiccup, a laugh they share,
While ducks in tuxedos float with flair.
Quacking out jokes as they paddle by,
Joining the mischief, oh me, oh my!

Sunsets giggle as colors blend,
Painting the sky, a shimmering trend.
In this liquid laughter, life takes flight,
With such silly songs, the world feels bright!

Verses of the Meandering Streamlet

A stream that trips over stones so small,
Gobbles up giggles, oh what a squall!
With every curve, it whispers a jest,
Who knew such waters could be so blessed!

Tadpoles in tuxes begin to prance,
Synchronized swimming, they take a chance.
With bulging eyes and serious flair,
As bubbles pop up, the fun is rare!

The pebbles hum, their voices unite,
In a wild concert, such sheer delight!
Bouncing along, they keep the beat,
Who knew such rocks could dance on their feet?

As night falls gently, the stars appear,
Winking and laughing, they draw us near.
Nature's own antics, a quirky dream,
In a world like this, we all can beam!

Poetic Currents of Twilight

Beneath the moon, shadows start to play,
Trees engage in a game, come what may.
They sway and bow with a wink and a grin,
Nature's own stage, let the fun begin!

A rabbit with spectacles, quite profound,
Reads funny stories as he hops around.
His friends gather close for a giggle spree,
In the twilight glow, all wild and free.

Ripples chuckle through the darkening tide,
As fireflies twinkle, stars by their side.
Each flicker a giggle, each glow a cheer,
In this quirky dance, nature draws near!

As the night deepens, the laughter flows,
In poetic currents where silliness grows.
Join in the fun, let your spirits lift,
In this twilight wonder, let joy be the gift!

Tranquility in the Water's Embrace

A fish named Fred in a little pond,
Danced with the leaves that floated beyond.
He twirled and he swirled in a watery spree,
While turtles just laughed, saying, "Look at he!"

The lily pads giggled, the frogs joined the fun,
They played leapfrog games in the warm summer sun.
With splashes and splutters, the day slipped away,
As ripples of laughter turned night into day.

The dragonflies buzzed with a cheeky delight,
They zipped through the twilight, oh, what a sight!
While minnows made faces that made the otters grin,
In tranquil embrace, let the hilarity begin!

Together they danced, oh what a parade,
In the coolness of night, where memories are made.
With whimsy and wonder, their worries erased,
In the calm of the water, they joyfully raced.

Currents of Reflection and Reverie

A duck with a hat and a wobbly gait,
Strolled down the stream, feeling quite great.
He quacked loud and proud, spreading jokes in the air,
While fish rolled their eyes, pretending not to care.

The rocks chimed in with a clatter and shout,
"Hey, take it easy, there's no need to pout!"
But humor cascaded like bubbles through foam,
While frogs perched atop, they felt at home.

A beaver with spectacles gnawed on a tree,
He said, "Laughing brings even logs like me!"
As shadows grew long on the water's blue face,
The laughter reflected in nature's embrace.

With giggles and gurgles, the current flowed free,
In a raucous ensemble of nature's jubilee.
From banks all around, the joy joined the stream,
As dreams danced together, afloat like a dream.

Whispers of the Waters

Bubbles ascended with giggles and squeaks,
While crayfish told tales with their tiny beaks.
The minnows chimed in with a splash and a spout,
As the river chuckled, there was never a doubt.

A warbler perched close, serenading the crew,
Singing silly songs under skies bright and blue.
The reeds swayed along, tapping feet in delight,
While the current carried on, bubbling with might.

A raccoon named Ray donned a crown made of leaves,
Conducted the giggles as the waterway weaves.
"With laughter aplenty, we'll brighten the day!"
The fishes agreed, in their own fishy way.

Through ripples and chuckles, the waters spoke light,
In a symphony soft under stars shining bright.
So come join the party, where humor's the drill,
And let it cascade like the whispers that thrill.

Echoes in a Stream

In the heart of the brook, a chorus arose,
With frogs on a log striking poet en rose.
They croaked clever verses to tickle the glee,
While chipmunks all jived, filled with joyous esprit.

An otter named Ollie played fetch with a shoe,
Cannonballing in with a splash as he flew.
The ripples rejoiced, while the waterbugs danced,
Scribbling in bubbles as the moments pranced.

The sun winked a smile, as the day drifted on,
With shadows all laughing at the antics bar none.
A turtle proclaimed, "Why walk when you glide?"
As splashes of giggles flowed side by side.

With whispers of joy that floated like mist,
The wild echoed laughter, how could one resist?
In the stream's gentle flow lies a tale that we've spun,
A playful reminder that life is pure fun.

Serenity in Motion

A snail wore his party hat,
He glided with style, imagine that!
He danced on a leaf, oh what a sight,
Practicing moves from morning to night.

The frogs cheered him on with a croak,
While a butterfly whispered a joke.
The breeze joined in with a swirl and a twirl,
As leaves did the limbo, all around they'd whirl.

But then came a gust, what a surprise!
The snail just laughed, no need for cries.
He flipped on his shell, a natural pro,
And surfed down the path, oh what a show!

At the end of the day, all were a-buzz,
"A snail's got the moves!" they all made a fuss.
With giggles and grins, the fun seemed so fair,
Life's little moments, oh how they compare!

The Lilt of the Liquid

In a pond so blue, sat a duck with a grin,
He quacked silly songs, singing out loud, not thin.
His feet gave a tap, on the lily pads flapping,
While fish joined the beat, with bubbles a-sapping.

The sun tossed a wink, in a twinkly way,
As frogs followed suit, providing the play.
They slipped and they slid, in the splish and the splash,
A chorus of laughter, oh what a bash!

A turtle rolled in, thinking he'd dance,
But instead took a spin, in a clumsy prance.
With bubbles all giggling, they cheered him so loud,
As he waved his flipper, feeling quite proud.

And when dusk drew near, with colors so bright,
The pond still held echoes of joy and delight.
They held a grand party, from dusk until dawn,
For the spirit of fun, remained ever so strong!

Over the Stones, a Song

A river began to hum, with pebbles that winked,
Each splash and each ripple, an inkling of sync.
The stones held their breaths, as if in a trance,
Wondering if waters could really dance.

The fish in their suits, with tails made of gold,
Jived along joyfully, as stories were told.
A turtle dropped by, flipping over a stone,
"Is this a singing stream, or am I just blown?"

It tickled the ends of the lily's long reach,
As laughter cascaded like waves to the beach.
Ripples expanded, with a giddy delight,
As rocks chuckled softly, from morning to night.

So over the stones, the sweet tune they made,
A symphony bright, in the sunlight that played.
Each note flew around, like a butterfly's wing,
While the joy of the moment was all they could bring.

Join the Jingle of the Flow

An otter on skates, what a curious sight,
Glided through puddles, oh what pure delight.
He wobbled a bit, then gave a loud cheer,
"Come join the fun, my friends, gather near!"

A beaver appeared, with a hat on his head,
"Let's build a grand slide, who needs a warm bed?"
The squirrels, they scattered, with giggles galore,
"Let's make this a bash, we can't ignore!"

With twigs and some leaves, they created a ramp,
And down they did fly, like a wild little stamp.
The splashes and shrieks filled the cool autumn air,
While joy danced around, without any care.

As twilight crept in, with stars shining bright,
The critters all gathered, what a jubilant sight!
With stories and laughter, they packed up to go,
But promised to return, to join in the flow!

Whispers of the Brook

In the shade where the waters play,
Fish share jokes in a splashy way.
The frogs croak tales, and the reeds sway,
While dragonflies dance the livelong day.

A turtle grins with a wink so sly,
As the ripples giggle and bubbles fly.
The old heron struts by with a sigh,
Saying, "Everyone's here, so let's get high!"

A leaf floats down with a comedic twist,
Joining the fun, it can't resist.
The water's a stage, not a drop missed,
Where every critter gets a chance to exist.

As twilight falls and the stars peep in,
The brook laughs softly, a cheeky grin.
With every splash, the joy begins,
Under the moonlight, nobody's thin.

Songs Beneath the Surface

Bubbles rise with a bubbly tune,
They're singing sweetly beneath the moon.
A fish flips out with a funky swoon,
While crabs dance hard, shaking their ruin.

Giggling minnows race here and there,
Composing sonnets with flair to spare.
The sand's a stage, and the currents care,
For all the melodies floating in air.

In the depths, where secrets lie,
Eels tell tales of a daring sky.
With every ripple, the stories fly,
Making everyone laugh and sigh.

The frog's solo is a hit by chance,
As the cattails sway, joining the dance.
A symphony born from a mischievous glance,
The water alive, in joyous romance.

Lullabies of the Stream

In the cradle of rocks, the water hums,
A sleepy tune where the laughter comes.
With splashes soft, the current drums,
While busy bugs beat out gentle thums.

The pebbles giggle, tickled by flow,
Sliding along, they put on a show.
A snail does a jig, moving far too slow,
While the tadpoles cheer, all lined in a row.

Between the banks where the grasses weep,
A family of otters start to leap.
With every dive, they make a sweep,
For underwater dreams, they want to keep.

As starlight glimmers on the stream's face,
The night becomes lively, a lively chase.
With giggles and gurgles, they find their place,
In nature's lullaby, a charming embrace.

Echoes in the Gentle Flow

Waves of laughter bounce all around,
From stony banks, to where fish are found.
Mirth floats high, while laughter resounds,
With ripples of joy, the world is crowned.

The old wise fish tells a zany tale,
As bubble buddy starts to flail.
While squirrels pause, leaning on a rail,
The stream calls out with a snickering wail.

Every plop is a punchline sweet,
Twisting the flow and moving the beat.
Where water and antics are destined to meet,
In this giggling dance, no one's discreet.

Silly stones hold secrets untold,
And every current has jokes to unfold.
The echoes of fun, like treasures of gold,
In the heartbeat of nature, both bold and old.

Whispered Wishes by Water

By the stream where wishes float,
Frogs in tuxes sing and gloat.
They croak their dreams with all their might,
While dragonflies buzz, taking flight.

A turtle snickers at the show,
As a fish takes a bow, moving slow.
The lily pads cheer, all aflutter,
While the mossy rocks crack jokes, and stutter.

The water's giggle dances near,
As bubbles pop, it's quite the cheer.
"Make a wish!" the brooklets tease,
While ripples ripple with such ease.

With every splash, there's laughter loud,
The pond's become a playful crowd.
Wishes whisper, hopes entwine,
In this watery world, it's simply divine!

Dialogues of the Deep

Beneath the waves, a clam cracks wise,
To a nearby shrimp with curious eyes.
"Why don't you join me for a dance?
The ocean's floor is ours to prance!"

A wise old crab chimes in with flair,
"Who needs a partner? I'm rich in hair!"
With a shrug, the shrimp just giggles,
As the seaweed sways and wriggles.

A grouchy eel reminds them all,
"Quit your nonsense, don't make me haul!"
But the fish all chuckle, flit and dart,
Creating chaos, a whirlpool of art.

They tumble and swirl, a dazzling scene,
In the currents of laughter, they reign supreme.
With each comical flick, and each little quip,
The dialogues echo, a whimsical trip.

The Fountain of Fables

In the park, a fountain sprays,
With tales of fish and froggy plays.
Squirrels gather, chattering loud,
While doves compete to stand out proud.

Water nymphs giggle, tales they weave,
Of mischief done on New Year's Eve.
Each splash tells a story, new and bright,
And the moon giggles at the sight.

A gnome pipes up, "I once knew a seal,
Who wore a top hat and danced with zeal!"
The fountain gurgles, "Really? Oh dear!
Next you'll say the cat was a deer!"

Fables flow like water free,
With every drop, more jesting glee.
The fountain chuckles, no one's serious,
In this world, all things are curious!

The River's Gentle Gesture

The river waves as it flows along,
Tickling stones with a gentle song.
It whispers secrets, hidden and sly,
While frogs compete for the best high guy.

A beaver hums with toothy grin,
Building his dam, a bubbly kin.
"Alright, who's got the next big plan?
Maybe a float for this good little man?"

A fish bubbles up, "Let's have a race!
Last one to the bend is a soggy face!"
With a plop and a splash, they're off to glide,
While water snakes laugh, in silly pride.

The river chuckles, a merry tease,
"Who needs a boat? Just ride the breeze!"
With currents twisting, laughter foams,
In this watery world, the fun just roams!

Streams of Serenity

A fish wore a hat, thought he'd be a star,
He danced in the water, swaying afar.
The frogs in the reeds laughed with delight,
As bubbles rose up, a comical sight.

The riverbank squirrels threw nuts in a race,
A splash and a dash, oh what a wild chase!
The current went crazy, spun round like a top,
While ducks quacked a tune, no one wanted to stop.

In twilight's embrace, a turtle snored loud,
He dreams of the waves in a whimsical crowd.
The ripples keep giggling, the pebbles jeer,
As the moonlight spills silver, it's time for good cheer.

So join the parade where the waters collide,
With laughter and joy, let your troubles slide.
We wade in the coolness, with splashes of fun,
In the streams of our heart, let the merriment run.

Life's Liquid Verse

A can of soda popped by the creek so bright,
It fizzed like our giggles, a bubbling flight.
The minnows were blushing, a tickle or two,
As we tossed out our wishes like clouds made of blue.

The willows all whispered a secret so sweet,
They danced with the breeze, got up on their feet.
With each little plop, the laughs took the stage,
While the crickets in chorus turned the next page.

Oh, splashes of joy are the best kind of rhyme,
As we skip down the shore, just killing some time.
Our toes kiss the water, each ripple a smile,
Life's precious moments, let's savor awhile.

So add to this story, with winks and with cheers,
Let's capture the giggles, drown out all our fears.
In this bubbly expanse, where the silly rivers flow,
We treasure each giggle, and let the world glow.

Cradle of the Brook

Upon a small rock sat a snail named Lou,
He wore mismatched socks, his favorite hue.
The waterwas laughing, the stones shared a grin,
As the brook whispered secrets that made us all spin.

Bubbles burst forth with giggles of glee,
A swirl and a swirl, it's a party at sea!
The frogs on the lily pads played leapfrog for fun,
While dragonflies danced, under mid-afternoon sun.

The old otter rolled over, a splash and a crash,
He snagged a big fish, all in a great flash!
But the fish wiggled free, gave a leap and a spin,
And with a sly grin, said, "Catch me again!"

So let's find the joy in this brookside delight,
With laughter and splashes that glow in the night.
In this cradle of chuckles, may we forever share,
A story of whimsy, in this water so rare.

The Mixing of Echoes

The echoes of laughter live deep in the stream,
Where turtles play hopscotch and fish chase a dream.
Each ripple a chuckle, each wave a bright smile,
The brook sings a tune that can travel a mile.

The clams hold a concert, each shell has a note,
A melody so silly you can't help but gloat.
The sunbeams all twinkle, like stars in the day,
As the whispers of water invite all to play.

The beavers are painting with strokes full of cheer,
While the ducks juggle rocks, oh what a career!
With each little splash, and a dance on the bank,
In the mixing of echoes, we find laughs to thank.

So gather your friends, let the giggles ignite,
In this whimsical haven, where the heart feels so light.
With winks and with splashes, let's float with the flow,
In the joy of our presence, together we glow.

www.ingramcontent.com/pod-product-compliance
Lightning Source LLC
Chambersburg PA
CBHW051639160426
43209CB00004B/714